love
those eyes

THIS BOOK IS FOR SOPHIE.

AN HACHETTE UK COMPANY
WWW.HACHETTE.CO.UK

FIRST PUBLISHED IN GREAT BRITAIN IN 2017 BY ILEX, A DIVISION OF
OCTOPUS PUBLISHING GROUP LTD
CARMELITE HOUSE, 50 VICTORIA EMBANKMENT, LONDON EC4Y 0DZ
WWW.OCTOPUSBOOKS.CO.UK

DESIGN, LAYOUT, AND TEXT COPYRIGHT © OCTOPUS PUBLISHING GROUP LIMITED 2017
ILLUSTRATIONS COPYRIGHT © ELISA MAZZONE 2017

ADDITIONAL PICTURE CREDITS: ELVIRA KONEVA/123RF.COM; ELVIRA KONEVA/DREAMSTIME.COM;
KADROF/DREAMSTIME.COM; SURASAK CH/SHUTTERSTOCK

DISTRIBUTED IN THE US BY HACHETTE BOOK GROUP
1290 AVENUE OF THE AMERICAS, 4TH AND 5TH FLOORS, NEW YORK, NY 10104

DISTRIBUTED IN CANADA BY CANADIAN MANDA GROUP
664 ANNETTE ST., TORONTO, ONTARIO, CANADA M6S 2C8

PUBLISHER: ROLY ALLEN
EDITORIAL DIRECTOR: ZARA LARCOMBE
MANAGING SPECIALIST EDITOR: FRANK GALLAUGHER
EDITOR: FRANCESCA LEUNG
ADMIN ASSISTANT: SARAH VAUGHAN
ART DIRECTOR: JULIE WEIR
DESIGNER: ELISA MAZZONE
PRODUCTION CONTROLLER: SARAH KULASEK-BOYD

LEMONBERRY SANS FONT USED COURTESY OF SABRINA SCHLEIGER
WWW.MONKEYROODLESFONTS.COM
FREELAND FONT USED COURTESY OF LAURA CONDOURIS
WWW.TRIALBYCUPCAKES.COM

ISBN 978-1-78157-496-6
A CIP CATALOGUE RECORD FOR THIS BOOK IS AVAILABLE FROM THE BRITISH LIBRARY.

PRINTED AND BOUND IN CHINA
10 9 8 7 6 5 4 3 2 1

love those eyes

ALLURING EYE-MAKEUP LOOKS FOR EVERY OCCASION

BY SARAH JANE ELLIS, ILLUSTRATED BY ELISA MAZZONE

ilex

contents

the foundations

Having worked as a professional makeup artist for many years I have had the pleasure of applying makeup for many different people. Every person I do makeup for is different and every set of eyes is unique, meaning that every look I have created has also been individual.

This sense of individuality is what has inspired me to produce a collection of eye-makeup looks so that you can choose one to suit you and your style, and one that is perfect for any occasion you have in mind. As a makeup artist, the most frequent question I am asked is how to do the eye-makeup for a certain event or look. In my experience every event calls for a different approach to your makeup, and the eye-makeup is often the foundation to create the rest of the look and also the centerpiece to it.

I hope that when a person picks up this book it encourages them to experiment and approach the makeup they do every day in a new and exciting way, regardless of their level of expertise—whether that's someone searching for a unique tutorial, or who wants to gain confidence by starting off with a more familiar look. Many people see the eyes as the window to the soul, so why not dress that window to impress? The art of makeup is one that can empower a person and the eyes are the best place to start. With Elisa's stunning illustrations, you'll find there are lots of looks you'll want to try, and by following the step-by-step guides, that they are easy to recreate too.

If you look through the designs and see something you like, feel free to adjust the colors to suit your skin tone as any professional makeup artist would do, and finish all suitable looks with your favorite mascara, or false lashes as you prefer. Once you have mastered the looks in this book, I also hope that you will continue to explore your personal makeup style by creating your own looks inspired by the ones featured here. The looks that I have created vary in difficulty but can be achieved by anyone with the right tools and patience.

So whether you are getting ready for a night on the town or need a work look to show you mean business, my mission is that you will find an eye-makeup look here that works for you. You are the artist and we want you to enjoy forging your own tailor-made look.

1. EYEBROW/BROW BONE

2. EYELID

3. UPPER LASHLINE

4. LASHES

5. UNDER-EYES

6. LOWER LASHLINE

7. WATERLINE

8. TEAR DUCT

tools

There are some essentials that I would recommend having in your makeup kit:

2 x BLENDING BRUSHES
Always have one blending brush to apply eyeshadow and one clean blending brush. Use the clean blending brush in gentle buffing motions to soften edges and blend colors together for a seamless finish.

FLAT SHADER BRUSH
Use this brush when you want a stronger color payoff, a patting motion is suitable for application.

PENCIL BRUSH
This brush is perfect for applying or blending eyeshadow or eyeliner along the lower lashline.

PIN-POINT CONCEALER BRUSH
Highlighting your tear duct is a breeze with this!

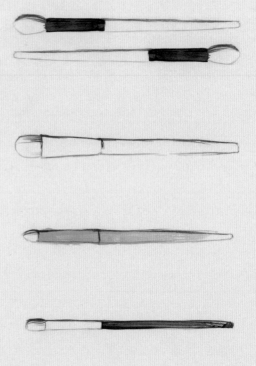

Other tools

* Disposable mascara wands/"spoolies" (elongated re-usable mascara wands)
* Adhesive tape
* Pencil sharpener
* Eyebrow brush/comb
* Makeup wipes/remover

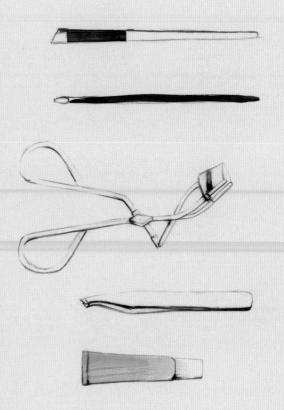

FLAT ANGLED BRUSH
Useful for filling in your brows, this brush can also be used for eyeliner.

PRECISE EYELINER BRUSH
As the name suggests, this brush is perfect for creating precise eyeliner.

EYELASH CURLER
Add extra drama to your lashes by curling them before adding mascara or applying false lashes.

TWEEZERS
These are helpful for applying false lashes and tidying up stray eyebrow hairs.

LATEX-FREE EYELASH GLUE
As well as for applying false lashes, this is useful for sticking gemstones or other small decorations to the face.

Materials checklist

ESSENTIALS

* Eyeshadow
* Mascara
* Concealer
* Eyeliner pens/pencils
* Colored cream bases

* Eye moisturizing cream
* Eye primer
* Translucent powder
* Highlighter powder

FINISHING TOUCHES

* False lashes
* Stickers
* Gemstones
* Glitter

Get prepped

It's important to achieve a good initial base with eye primer before applying your eye-makeup so that your look lasts longer. Here's how to do it!

1. Apply a suitable hydrating eye cream under your eyes.

2. Pluck any stray hairs from your eyebrows and style your eyebrows as you desire.

3. Add translucent eye primer over the eyelid, along the lower lashline, and up to the brow bone.

cheat sheet

Over the years, I have picked up many tips to make life a lot easier when it comes to applying makeup. Here are some of the best ones that can save time and hassle, and give a finish worthy of a pro.

* If you are creating a dramatic makeup look, apply your eye-makeup first to avoid ruining your foundation if eyeshadow drops down onto your face.

* Use adhesive tape as a masking-off guide to help create the perfect winged eyeliner line, or more bold looks such as the "cat eye."

* Glide a light beige eyeliner along the waterline if you wish your eyes to look bigger.

* Use concealer on a flat eyeliner brush to touch up or sharpen edges after you've drawn them.

* Remove any glitter fallout with adhesive tape.

* Apply eyeshadow in light layers, adding more gradually to avoid going off course.

* Use a white cream base first to intensify any eyeshadow.

* If you would prefer a softer finish, use brown eyeliner instead of black.

* Use waterproof mascara on the lower eyelashes to avoid "panda eyes."

* In the case of not having a steady hand, use gel eyeliner instead of liquid for more control.

* Use a synthetic brush with any cream products, as the brush is much easier to clean afterward.

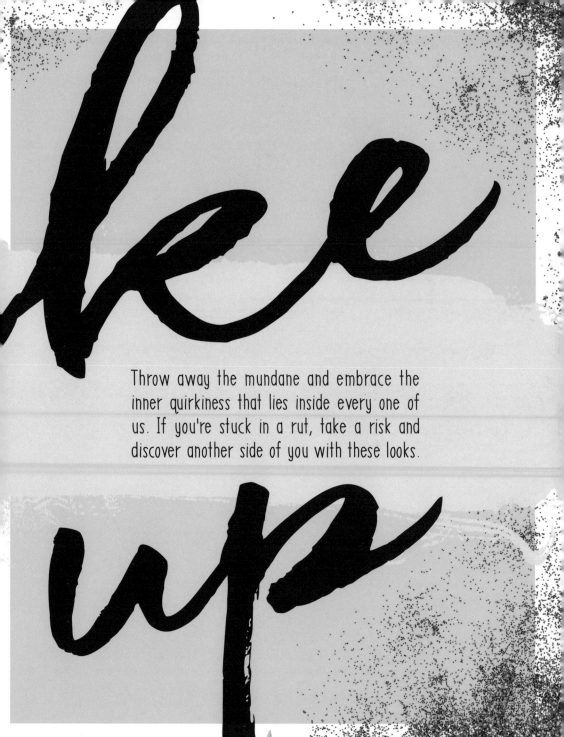

like

up

Throw away the mundane and embrace the inner quirkiness that lies inside every one of us. If you're stuck in a rut, take a risk and discover another side of you with these looks.

date night

1. Buff light brown eyeshadow into and above the crease.

2. Buff dark brown eyeshadow into and above the crease.

3. Pat black eyeshadow over the eyelid and blend any harsh edges. Add a thick line of dark purple eyeshadow along the upper lashline.

4. Run black eyeliner along the waterline and blend dark purple eyeshadow along the lower lashline.

5. Add mascara or false lashes to complete the look if you wish.

1

2

3

4

5

1

4

2

5

3

1. Apply dark grape eyeshadow to the outer corner and crease of the eye.

2. Add shimmer peach eyeshadow to the center of the eyelid.

3. Blend an eyeshadow that matches your skin tone onto the inner corner of the eyelid.

4. Create a black eyeliner flick and add white eyeliner to the waterline. Blend any harsh edges and add some dark grape eyeshadow along the outer part of the lower lashline.

5. Add mascara or false lashes to complete the look if you wish.

raspberry fizz

I am
unique

miami vibes

1. Buff peach eyeshadow over the eyelid and into the crease.

2. Pat shimmer copper eyeshadow over the eyelid.

3. Buff matt dark brown eyeshadow into the outer corner of the eyelid and up into the crease.

4. Highlight the tear duct with an iridescent blue eyeshadow and apply black liquid eyeliner along the upper lashline.

5. Buff dark brown eyeshadow along the lower lashline. Add mascara or false lashes to complete the look if you wish.

1

4

2

5

3

1

2

3

4

5

6

SHAKE IT UP

heat wave

1. Buff pumpkin orange eyeshadow into the crease.

2. Apply red rust eyeshadow along the crease line.

3. With a smaller brush, apply mahogany eyeshadow over the red rust eyeshadow.

4. With a flat damp brush apply cream-colored eyeshadow to the eyelid.

5. Create a dramatic flick with black eyeliner.

6. Add white eyeliner to the waterline and red rust eyeshadow to the lower lashline. Add mascara or false lashes to complete the look if you wish.

A bronzed face and nude glossy lips will complement these eyes.

bad influence

1. Buff black cream base over the eyelid and into and above the crease.

2. Pat a shimmer purple eyeshadow onto the inner corner.

3. Pat a darker shimmer purple eyeshadow onto the center of the eyelid and blend any strong edges.

4. Glide black pencil eyeliner onto the waterline and apply dark blue eyeshadow along the lower lashline. Add mascara or false lashes to complete the look if you wish.

+ Dust loose translucent powder that matches your skin tone, under the eye to catch any eyeshadow fallout. Brush away when finished!

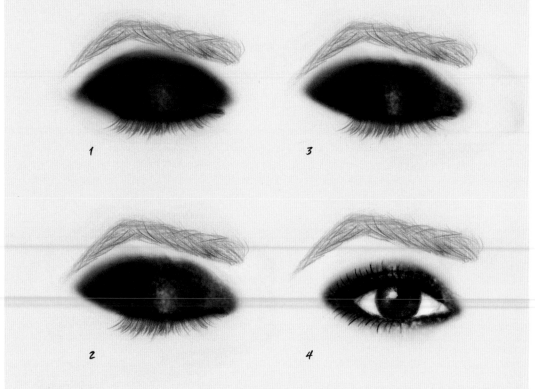

1

3

2

4

gold extravagance

1   2

1. Buff a subtle peach eyeshadow
   into the crease and pat gold
   shimmer eyeshadow onto
   the eyelid and tear duct.

2. Buff matt dark brown
   eyeshadow onto the outer
   corner of the eye and
   blend up into the crease.

3. Blend dark brown eyeliner
   along the lower lashline.

4. Apply black liquid eyeliner
   along the upper lashline and
   glide black pencil eyeliner
   along the waterline. Add
   mascara or false lashes to
   complete the look if you wish.

3

4

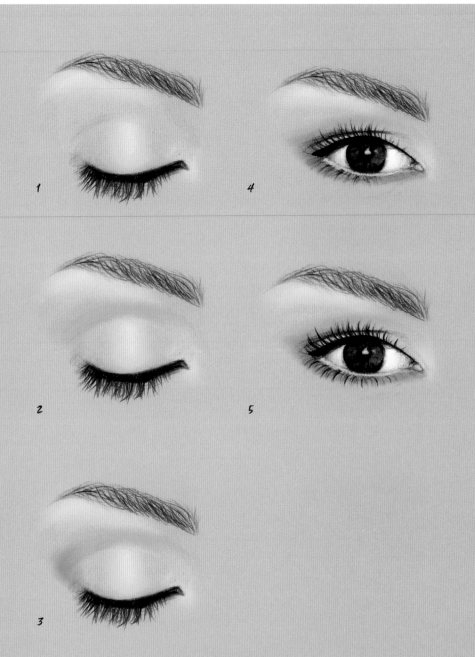

1

2

3

4

5

SHAKE IT UP

pretty petal

1. Apply satin peach eyeshadow over the eyelid and highlight the tear duct with a lighter shade of eyeshadow.

2. Buff pale pink eyeshadow into and above the crease.

3. Add lavender eyeshadow to the outer corner of the eyelid and along the lower lashline. Blend any strong edges.

4. Apply black liquid eyeliner along the upper lashline.

5. Add mascara or false lashes to complete the look if you wish.

I embrace
change

sherbert drop

1

2

3

1. Buff pink eyeshadow over the eyelid and into and above the crease.

2. Blend green eyeshadow along the lower lashline and highlight the tear duct with silver glitter.

3. Glide black pencil eyeliner along the waterline. Add mascara or false lashes to complete the look if you wish.

cloudburst

1. Buff a muddy brown eyeshadow over the eyelid.

2. Apply the same muddy brown eyeshadow along the lower lashline. Line the upper and lower lashlines and the waterline with black pencil eyeliner.

3. Buff over the eyeliner with a small brush (pencil brush) to create a smudged look. Add mascara or false lashes to complete the look if you wish.

1

2

3

spice of life

1. Apply pink-red eyeshadow along the crease and outward in a flick.

2. Buff highlighter into the tear duct and up into the pink-red.

3. Pat bronze eyeshadow over the eyelid.

4. Apply black liquid eyeliner to the upper lashline and make a flick. Buff pink-red eyeshadow along the lower lashline and glide black pencil eyeliner along the waterline. Add mascara or false lashes to complete the look if you wish.

1

3

2

4

eleg

ant
accent

Simplicity is the key here—these looks are fantastic for the beginner or people who want a striking and clean-cut look for every occasion. Each one of these unique looks is perfect for someone limited on time who still wants to turn heads wherever they go.

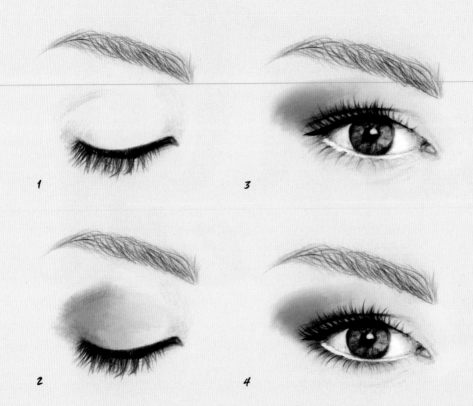

1

2

3

4

ELEGANT ACCENT

bright idea

1. Pat matt light gray eyeshadow over the inner half of the eyelid.

2. Apply a soft gray eyeshadow over the outer half of the eyelid and blend any harsh edges.

3. Glide black liquid eyeliner onto the upper lashline and white pencil eyeliner onto the waterline.

4. Use the same soft gray eyeshadow along the lower lashline. Add mascara or false lashes to complete the look if you wish.

pink flamingo

1. Apply a pale cream base over the eyelid.

2. Pat a baby pink eyeshadow over the eyelid leaving the inner corner blank.

3. Buff a dark gray eyeshadow onto the outer corner of the eyelid and into the crease to create a C shape.

4. Blend any harsh edges and create a small winged eyeliner on the upper lashline using black eyeliner.

5. Apply white eyeliner to the waterline and blend some dark gray eyeshadow along the lower lashline. Add mascara or false lashes to complete the look if you wish.

ELEGANT ACCENT

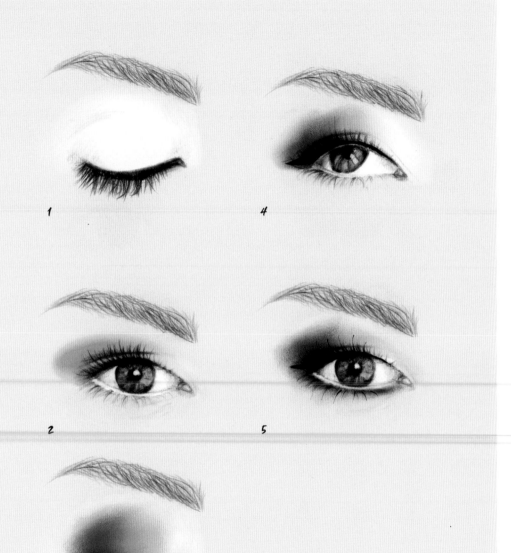

1

2

3

4

5

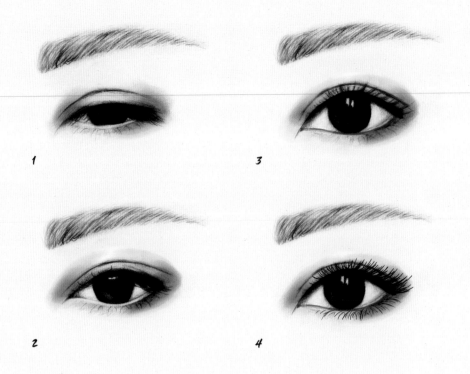

1

2

3

4

ELEGANT ACCENT

+ Use at least two coats of mascara for an editorial edge fit for the pages of a magazine.

1. Apply blue eyeshadow to the inner corner of the eyelid and the outer corner of the eye in a reverse C shape.

2. Pat a lighter blue eyeshadow onto the center of the eyelid and along the inner part of the lower lashline. Blend any harsh edges.

3. Add navy blue eyeliner to the waterline and black liquid eyeliner to the upper lashline.

4. Add mascara or false lashes to complete the look if you wish.

vacation blues

I am
effortless

The eye gloss gives the eyes a glazed look,
—it's like lipgloss but for the eyes.
You can use clear petroleum jelly for this too.

ELEGANT ACCENT

glazy days

1. Apply blue cream base over the eyelid, extending out to a side V at the outer corner.

2. Glide over the blue cream base with clear eye gloss.

3. Add mascara or false lashes to complete the look if you wish.

halo
heart

1. Buff pale pink eyeshadow along and above the crease.

2. Apply purple eyeshadow along the crease.

3. Add deep fuchsia eyeshadow to the inner and outer corners of the eye and along the lower lashline.

4. Apply black liquid eyeliner along the upper lashline and black pencil eyeliner along the waterline. Add mascara or false lashes to complete the look if you wish.

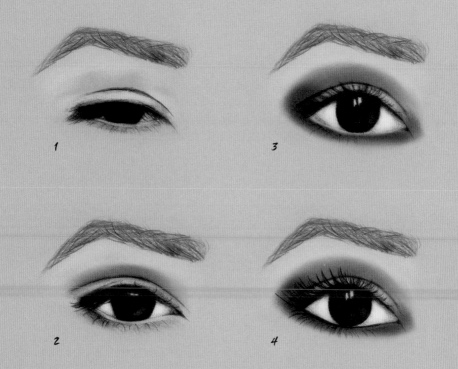

1

2

3

4

5

6

ELEGANT ACCENT

tutti frutti

1. Buff a pale pink eyeshadow into and above the crease.

2. Buff a dusty rose eyeshadow into the crease.

3. Pat yellow eyeshadow onto the inner corner of the eye.

4. Pat orange eyeshadow onto the rest of the eyelid and blend any harsh edges.

5. Buff black eyeshadow onto the outer corner of the eye.

6. Add a thin line to the upper lashline using black pencil eyeliner and also apply black pencil eyeliner to the waterline. Add mascara or false lashes to complete the look if you wish.

+ Before you start, you can apply eye primer and dust some translucent powder over it, to help eyeshadows blend more smoothly on top.

1

3

2

4

top notch

5

6

1. Pat a soft gray eyeshadow onto the eyelid and blend peach eyeshadow into the crease.

2. Highlight the tear duct with yellow eyeshadow.

3. Apply black liquid eyeliner to the upper lashline and create a flick.

4. Continue the black liquid eyeliner in a thin line down along the lower lashline. Glide white pencil eyeliner along the waterline.

5. Buff dark brown eyeshadow along the lower lashline to up above the flick.

6. Add mascara or false lashes to complete the look if you wish.

ELEGANT ACCENT

1

2

1. Add green liquid eyeliner
   to the upper lashline and
   create a small flick.

2. Run white eyeliner through
   the eyebrow.

3. Brush through the eyebrow
   with ice blue mascara. Add
   mascara to the lashes or
   add false lashes to complete
   the look if you wish.

3

match made

➕ Use a disposable mascara wand to brush through your eyebrows. If you use your regular mascara wand, you'll risk getting product into the wand and then into the mascara tube.

ELEGANT ACCENT

clowning around

1. Apply black liquid eyeliner
   along the upper lashline and
   create small triangles in the
   black liquid eyeliner.

2. Glide white pencil eyeliner
   along the waterline. Add
   mascara or false lashes to
   complete the look if you wish.

ELEGANT ACCENT

1

2

Practice is the key to success here. Draw the outlines of the triangles first and then fill them in, to ensure the edges are sharp.

1

2

3

ELEGANT ACCENT

linear love

1. Apply highlighter to the brow bone and tear duct.

2. Apply blue liquid eyeliner to the upper lashline and extend the line to create a small flick.

3. Add mascara or false lashes to complete the look if you wish.

+ Rest your elbow on the table to help keep your hand steady for a perfect line.

I radiate beauty and grace

darl

You'll be red carpet ready everywhere you go with these bold exciting looks. Turn every sidewalk into a catwalk and get those paparazzi snapping away.

drama
ing

first *dance*

1. Blend beige eyeshadow over the eyelid and apply highlighter to the brow bone and tear duct.

2. Buff matt brown eyeshadow onto the outer part of the eyelid and blend any harsh edges.

3. Glide black pencil eyeliner along the outer parts of the upper and lower lashlines. Glide white eyeliner along the waterline.

4. Blend all edges. Add mascara or false lashes to complete the look if you wish.

Add some glitter to the tear duct for extra sparkle.

1

3

2

4

standing ovation

1

2

3

4

1. Pat metallic silver eyeshadow onto the eyelid to above the crease.

2. Apply black gel eyeliner along the upper lashline and extend the line up to outline the shape of the silver eyeshadow.

3. Buff purple eyeshadow into and above the crease and blend.

4. Run white eyeliner along the waterline and blend gray eyeshadow along the lower lashline. Add gemstones around the eye for extra effect. Also add mascara or false lashes to complete the look if you wish.

You can replace the gems here with dots of metallic liquid eyeliner instead.

center stage

1. Apply metallic silver eyeshadow over the eyelid and pat silver glitter onto the center.

2. Buff a soft gray eyeshadow into the outer part of the crease and along the lower lashline. Blend any harsh edges.

3. Add mascara or false lashes to complete the look if you wish.

1

2

3

1

3

2

4

gold reign

DRAMA DARLING

5

6

1. Apply a super-shimmer gold eyeshadow over the eyelid.

2. Buff gray eyeshadow into the crease.

3. Buff a dark purple eyeshadow onto the outer corner of the eyelid to a point shape.

4. Apply black liquid eyeliner to the upper lashline to create a dramatic flick.

5. Blend any harsh edges and run the same gold eyeshadow along the lower lashline.

6. Add a soft brown eyeliner along the waterline. Add mascara or false lashes to complete the look if you wish.

I am
fearless

Make sure the black eyeshadow you use is matt for ultimate drama, as it will make the eyes look deeper, whereas if you use a shimmer shadow light will bounce off it.

1. Pat sand-beige eyeshadow onto the eyelid.

2. Buff black eyeshadow onto the outer part of the eyelid and extend the shadow out and up along the crease.

3. Blend black eyeliner along the lower lashline to meet with the outer part of the eyelid.

4. Apply black liquid eyeliner along the upper lashline, and black pencil eyeliner along the waterline, creating a point at the tear duct.

5. Add mascara or false lashes to complete the look if you wish.

animal instinct

1

4

2

5

3

DRAMA DARLING

waking hour

1. Apply vibrant blue eyeshadow to the outer half of the eye to create an extended side V shape.

2. Buff dark gray eyeshadow over the edge of the blue on the outer upper part of the eyelid and blend any harsh edges.

3. Blend white eyeshadow onto the inner corner of the eye and extend the shadow up to the brow bone.

4. Add black pencil eyeliner to the waterline and line the whole eye with a thick line of black liquid eyeliner, creating a flick. Add mascara or false lashes to complete the look if you wish.

Clean up around the blue eyeshadow with a cotton bud dipped in makeup remover for a stronger edge.

DRAMA DARLING

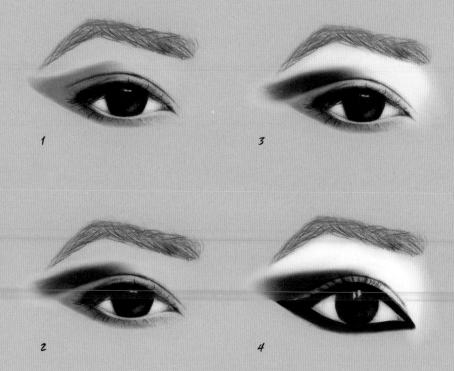

1

3

2

4

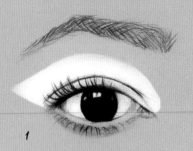

1

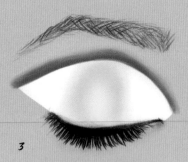

3

2

4

major crush

DRAMA DARLING

5

6

1. With white eyeliner create an extended pointed wave shape over the eyelid.

2. Buff dark brown eyeshadow onto the top edge of the white and blend it.

3. Pat blue eyeshadow onto the center of the eyelid.

4. Pat dark blue eyeshadow over the white eyeliner on the outer part of the eyelid.

5. Buff black eyeshadow onto the outer corner of the eyelid. Line the upper and lower lashlines and the waterline in black liquid eyeliner. Then outline the pointed wave shape over the eyelid in black liquid eyeliner too. Blend black eyeshadow along the lower lashline.

6. Add mascara or false lashes to complete the look if you wish.

1. Buff ice green eyeshadow along and above the crease.

2. Pat mint green eyeshadow onto the eyelid and apply highlighter to the brow bone.

3. Create a flick with silver glitter eyeliner on the upper lashline.

4. Apply black liquid eyeliner along the upper lashline then up and along the outline of the glitter.

5. Glide black pencil eyeliner along the waterline.

6. Add mascara or false lashes to complete the look if you wish.

princess cut

1

2

3

4

5

6

goddess rising

1. Apply white cream base to the inner half of the eyelid.

2. Apply blue cream base to the outer half of the eye.

3. Pat matching eyeshadows over the cream bases and blend them together.

4. Run white pencil eyeliner along the lower lashline and along the waterline.

5. Add black liquid eyeliner to the upper lashline and dab some chunky glitter under the eyes. Add mascara or false lashes to complete the look if you wish.

1

4

2

5

3

I shine everywhere I go

1

2

3

4

5

6

DRAMA DARLING

neon night

1. Apply a pale eyeshadow onto the eyelid up to the eyebrow.

2. Add a tropical blue eyeshadow onto the inner corner of the eyelid.

3. Buff a neon green eyeshadow onto the center of the eyelid.

4. Buff black eyeshadow onto the outer corner of the eyelid and blend any harsh edges.

5. With black liquid eyeliner outline the shape of the eyeshadow on the eyelid and also line the upper lashline.

6. Finish with black pencil eyeliner on the waterline and lower lashline to create a point at the tear duct. Add mascara or false lashes to complete the look if you wish.

busi

Got an important meeting or presentation you need to wow at? These looks will definitely bag you that deal. The makeup will be your armor as you step into the battlefield that is business.

ness
in mind

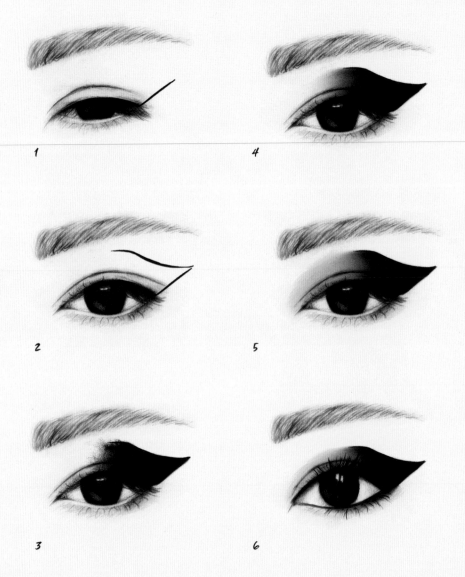

1

2

3

4

5

6

black sails

1. Use black gel eyeliner on the upper lashline and extend the line up half an inch toward the end of the eyebrow.

2. Extend the end of the line back across up under the brow bone.

3. Fill the contained space of the wing shape and outer half of the eyelid with a matt black eyeshadow.

4. Apply dark gray eyeshadow to the middle of the eyelid and blend it into the black.

5. Use a lighter gray eyeshadow on the inner corner of the eyelid and blend it into the dark gray.

6. Add black pencil eyeliner to the waterline and upper and lower lashlines, blending any harsh edges. Add mascara or false lashes to complete the look if you wish.

+ Don't forget you can use tape to help create this look more easily.

I will
conquer
the day

molten black

1. Gently buff deep dark brown eyeshadow into the inner and outer corners of the eyelid up to the crease.

2. Apply matt black eyeshadow to the tips of the inner and outer corners of the eyelid.

3. Pat a gold shimmer eyeshadow onto the center of the eyelid.

4. Add black eyeliner to the upper and lower lashlines and waterline. Add mascara or false lashes to complete the look if you wish.

✚ Take this look from day to night by accessorizing with gold jewelry for that red carpet look.

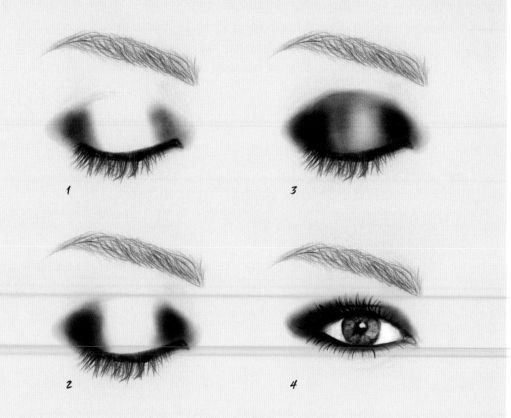

1

3

2

4

invitation only

1. Buff a sandy brown eyeshadow over the eyelid and above the crease.

2. Apply a soft brown eyeshadow over the eyelid.

3. Buff matt dark purple eyeshadow onto the outer corner of the eye and blend it into the crease.

4. Buff matt dark purple eyeshadow onto the outer part of the lower lashline and glide white eyeliner onto the waterline. Add mascara or false lashes to complete the look if you wish.

1

3

2

4

deadline

1. Pat purple-gray eyeshadow over the eyelid and above the crease. Blend the edges.

2. Buff brown eyeshadow onto the outer part of the eyelid and blend the edges.

3. Apply highlighter to the tear duct and brow bone and apply a shimmer dark purple eyeshadow onto the center of the eyelid.

4. Add black pencil eyeliner onto the outer part of the upper lashline and blend brown eyeliner along the lower lashline.

5. Glide cream-colored pencil eyeliner along the waterline. Add mascara or false lashes to complete the look if you wish.

If you don't have a highlighter to hand, you can use a lighter shade of eyeshadow or lighter shimmer eyeshadow instead.

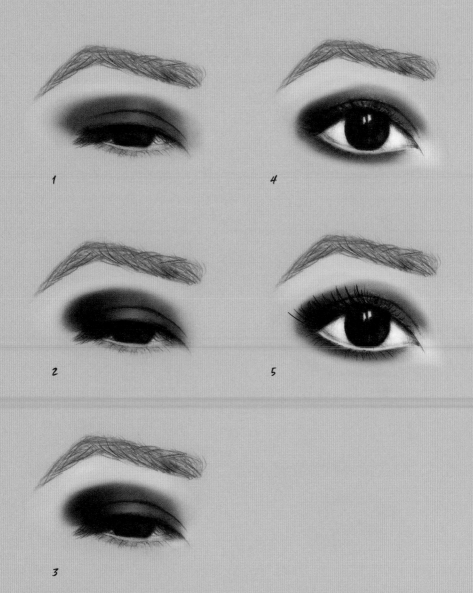

1

2

3

4

5

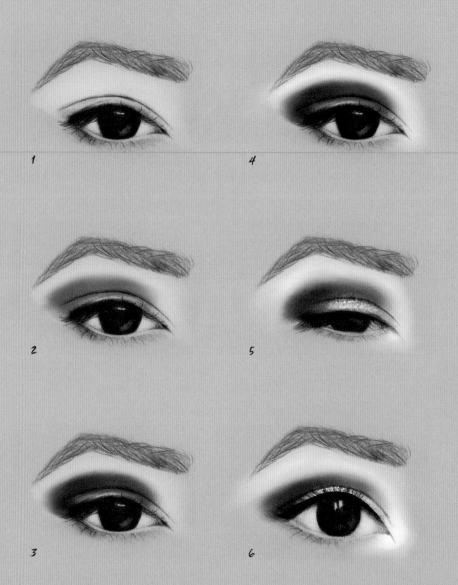

1

4

2

5

3

6

7

1. Buff neutral eyeshadow
   (a shade that matches
   your skin tone) over the
   whole eye and add a bright
   highlighter across the eyelid
   and up to the brow bone.

2. Buff a shimmer taupe
   eyeshadow onto the outer
   corner of the eye and along
   and above the crease.

3. Apply a dark brown eyeshadow
   over the shimmer taupe and
   blend any strong edges.

4. Add a bright highlighter to the
   tear duct and lightly blend
   it up to the brow bone.

5. Dab gold glitter onto the
   center of the eyelid.

6. Apply black liquid eyeliner
   to the upper lashline.

7. Buff light gray eyeshadow
   along the lower lashline. Add
   mascara or false lashes to
   complete the look if you wish.

limited edition

1

3

2

4

ace
of spades

5

6

1. Apply light burnt-orange eyeshadow onto the crease.

2. Add dark burnt-orange eyeshadow onto the crease.

3. Pat gray eyeshadow onto the eyelid.

4. Buff dark purple eyeshadow into the outer corner of the eyelid.

5. Apply black liquid eyeliner to the upper lashline to create a flick.

6. Add black eyeliner pencil along the waterline and buff blue eyeshadow along the lower lashline. Add mascara or false lashes to complete the look if you wish.

You can use translucent powder to take away shine from skin or over makeup to set it. It has no pigment and will suit any skin tone.

1. Pat a medium-shimmer gold eyeshadow over the eyelid.

2. Buff matt pink eyeshadow over the crease and along the inner part of the lower lashline.

3. Blend a matt soft dark brown eyeshadow onto the outer corner of the eye and into the crease.

4. Create a thin flick with black liquid eyeliner on the upper lashline and lightly buff soft brown eyeshadow along the outer part of the lower lashline.

5. Glide a white pencil eyeliner along the waterline. Add mascara or false lashes to complete the look if you wish.

kitten heel

1

4

2

5

3

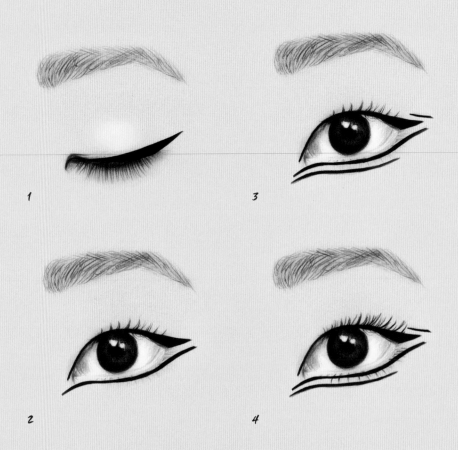

1

3

2

4

Glide a metallic silver or gold
eyeliner between the lines for
a more futuristic look.

in the zone

1. Glide black liquid eyeliner along the upper lashline and create a flick.

2. Line the lower lashline with black eyeliner, extending the line out to under the tear duct and toward the temple.

3. Add another shorter line underneath the lower lashline and make a dash above the upper lashline flick.

4. Add mascara or false lashes to complete the look if you wish.

creative director

✚ Add more dots along the lower
lashline for a more unusual look.

1. Blend a neutral shimmer
   eyeshadow (a shade
   matching your skin tone)
   over the eyelid.

2. Add black liquid eyeliner to
   the upper lashline and extend
   the line to create a flick.

3. Add a dot of black liquid
   eyeliner to the center of the
   lower lashline. Add mascara
   or false lashes to complete
   the look if you wish.

1

2

1. Add a thick line of black liquid eyeliner along the upper lashline and create a flick.

2. Apply a thin line of lavender liquid eyeliner along the upper lashline, that hugs the black eyeliner.

3. Add mascara or false lashes to complete the look if you wish.

3

signature

+ Keep lashes separated for maximum impact. "Spoolies" are good for this. You can use disposable mascara wands, but spoolies can be cleaned and re-used.

I am the
architect
of my life

wil

chi

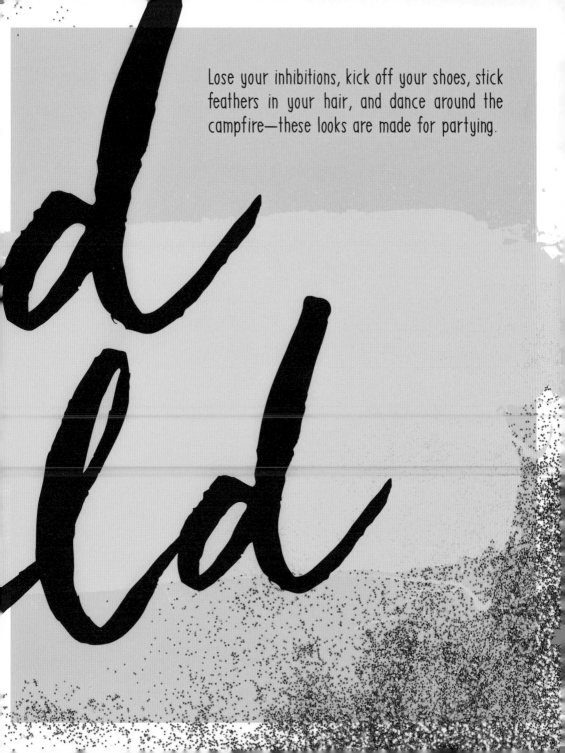

Lose your inhibitions, kick off your shoes, stick feathers in your hair, and dance around the campfire—these looks are made for partying.

eden's promise

7

1. Add white eyeshadow to the tear duct and pat light green eyeshadow next to it up to the crease.

2. Pat a slightly darker green eyeshadow onto the center of the eyelid.

3. Add dark green eyeshadow onto the outer part of the eyelid.

4. Buff deep dark green eyeshadow onto the outer edge of the dark green, and create a point at the outer corner of the eyelid.

5. Outline the eyeshadows and tear duct with a jagged line using black liquid eyeliner.

6. Add lines in different thicknesses across the eyelid in black liquid eyeliner to give a cracked effect.

7. Glide black pencil eyeliner along the waterline and lower lashline. Add mascara or false lashes to complete the look if you wish.

1

4

2

5

3

+ Add some translucent powder under the lower black line of eyeliner to stop it from bleeding.

kingfisher

1. Buff brown eyeshadow into and above the crease.

2. Pat green eyeshadow onto the eyelid.

3. Apply yellow eyeliner to the inner corner of the lower lashline.

4. Add black liquid eyeliner to the upper lashline and create a small flick. Extend this line down along the lower lashline to outline the yellow eyeliner.

5. Buff brown eyeshadow along the lower lashline. Add blue eyeliner to the waterline. Add mascara or false lashes to complete the look if you wish.

I am
wild
and free

purrfect

1. Add highlighter to the brow bone and blend mustard yellow eyeshadow over the eyelid.

2. Add brown eyeliner along the lower lashline.

3. Add brown eyeliner along the waterline.

4. With black liquid eyeliner add various-sized dots along the upper lashline, creating the shape of a line of eyeliner with a flick.

5. Add mascara or false lashes to complete the look if you wish.

+ If you wear eyeshadow without a primer, after a few hours you may notice the eyeshadow has moved into the crease of your eyelid. Dust translucent powder over the completed look to prevent this.

1

4

2

5

3

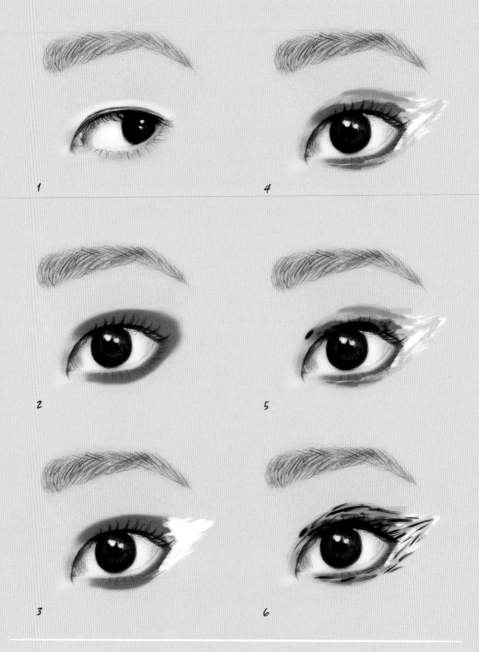

going rogue

7

1. Add a white cream base to the eyelid, add highlighter to the tear duct, and add matt yellow eyeshadow to the inner corner of the eye.

2. Buff pink eyeshadow over the eyelid and along the lower lashline to meet the yellow.

3. Add strokes of white eyeliner to the pink eyeshadow at the outer corner of the eye to create a feathery tail effect.

4. Create highlights around the eye and on the white eyeliner with strokes of yellow and orange eyeliners.

5. Using a mascara wand, dab small strokes of black mascara onto the center of the eyelid.

6. With black liquid eyeliner add dashes of black onto the design.

7. Glide black eyeliner along the upper lashline and waterline. Finish by adding silver glitter to the tear duct. Add mascara to the lashes or add false lashes to complete the look if you wish.

1

2

3

4

5

6

WILD CHILD

7

1. Buff matt pale-pink eyeshadow into and above the crease.

2. Buff matt bright-pink eyeshadow into and above the crease.

3. Pat indigo eyeshadow onto the inner corner of the eyelid.

4. Pat purple eyeshadow onto the outer corner of the eyelid and blend any harsh edges.

5. Run orange eyeliner along the lower lashline.

6. Run yellow eyeliner along the waterline.

7. Add black liquid eyeliner along the upper lashline and make a small flick. Add mascara or false lashes to complete the look if you wish.

tropical twist

glamping ground

1. Buff a soft dusky pink eyeshadow into and above the crease.

2. Buff bright red eyeshadow onto the outer corner of the eyelid.

3. Pat gold shimmer eyeshadow onto the inner corner and center of the eyelid.

4. Buff matt black eyeshadow onto the tip of the outer corner of the eyelid and blend any harsh edges.

5. Run bold blue eyeliner along the waterline.

6. Blend lilac eyeshadow along the lower lashline. Add mascara or false lashes to complete the look if you wish.

+ You can use a red blusher if you don't have a red eyeshadow to hand.

1

2

3

4

5

6

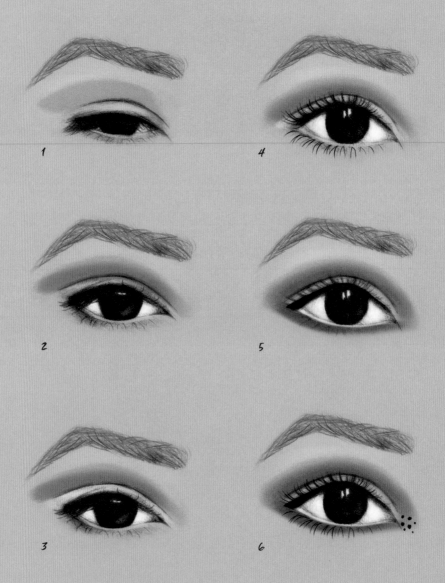

1

2

3

4

5

6

WILD CHILD

show-off

1. Apply burnt yellow eyeshadow into and above the crease.

2. Buff burnt orange eyeshadow into the crease.

3. Apply a soft white pencil eyeliner over the whole eyelid.

4. Pat matt yellow eyeshadow all over the eyelid on top of the white eyeliner.

5. Glide white eyeliner along the waterline and buff burnt orange eyeshadow along the lower lashline.

6. Highlight the tear duct with a pale yellow eyeshadow and add small dots to it with black liquid eyeliner. Add mascara or false lashes to complete the look if you wish.

1

2

3

4

5

6

cosmic pop

1. Apply highlighter to the brow bone and blend pale pink eyeshadow over the eyelid.

2. Add some star stickers around the eye.

3. Pat dark purple eyeshadow over and around the stickers.

4. Remove the stickers and blend the edges of the purple into the skin.

5. Apply highlighter to the tear duct and add black liquid eyeliner to the upper lashline, extending the line out to make a flick. Line the lower lashline with black eyeliner, mirroring the shape of the top eyeliner.

6. Add yellow eyeliner in between the lines of black eyeliner at the outer corner of the eye.

7. Glide blue pencil eyeliner along the waterline. Add mascara or false lashes to complete the look if you wish.

I live
in the
moment

1

2

3

4

5

double take

1. Buff a soft matt peach eyeshadow into and above the crease.

2. Pat a super-shimmer gold eyeshadow over the eyelid and blend any harsh edges.

3. Apply black liquid eyeliner along the upper lashline and draw a line with a flick on the crease above it.

4. Apply black eyeliner to the waterline and black liquid eyeliner along the lower lashline to create a point at the tear duct.

5. Add mascara or false lashes to complete the look if you wish.

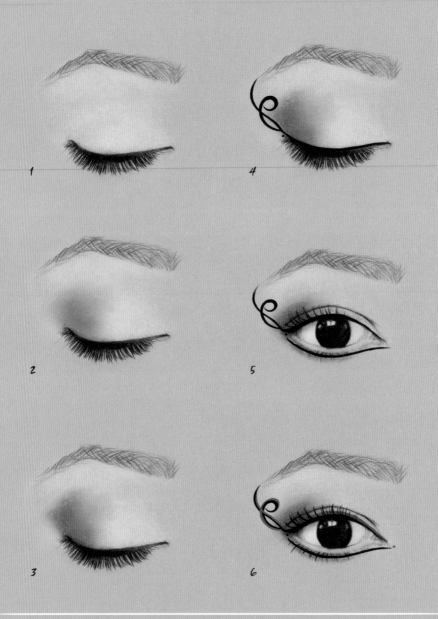

1

2

3

4

5

6

introducing

1. Apply champagne shimmer eyeshadow over the eyelid.

2. Buff soft brown eyeshadow over the outer half of the eyelid.

3. Buff purple eyeshadow over the outer half of the eyelid.

4. Glide black liquid eyeliner along the upper lashline and create two swirls extending up to the end of the eyebrow. Add a small dot at the outer corner of the eye in black liquid eyeliner too.

5. Line just under the lower lashline with black gel eyeliner.

6. Outline the black eyeliner and swirls on the upper lashline in blue liquid eyeliner, and add a dot to the tear duct in the blue liquid eyeliner. Add mascara or false lashes to complete the look if you wish.

✚ *Experiment with your own swirls and colors! You can create the look on both eyes or just one.*

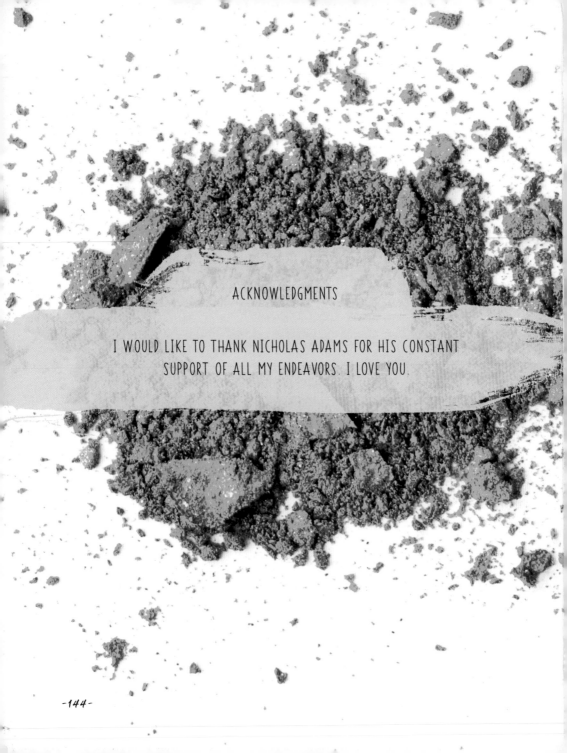

ACKNOWLEDGMENTS

I WOULD LIKE TO THANK NICHOLAS ADAMS FOR HIS CONSTANT
SUPPORT OF ALL MY ENDEAVORS. I LOVE YOU.